D1111924

SPIRIT GUIDES

3 Easy Steps To Connecting And Communicating
With Your Spirit Helpers

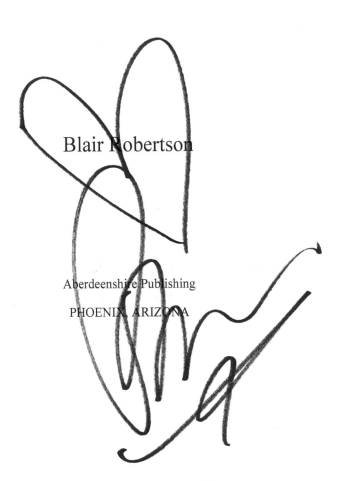

Blair Robertson

Aberdeenshire Publishing

PHOENIX, ARIZONA

Aberdeenshire Publishing
Box 1306
Litchfield Park, Arizona 85340

The information presented herein represents the view of the author as of the date of publication. Because of the rate with which conditions change, the author reserves the right to alter and update his opinion based on the new conditions. This is for informational purposes only. While every attempt has been made to verify the information provided in this report, neither the author nor his affiliates/partners assume any responsibility for errors, inaccuracies or omissions. Any slights of people or organizations are unintentional. If advice concerning legal or related matters is needed, the services of a fully qualified professional should be sought. Contents are not intended for use as a source of legal or accounting advice. You should be aware of any laws that govern business transactions or other business practices in your country and state. Any reference to any person or business whether living or dead is purely coincidental. Hug an attorney today.

Book Layout © 2014 BookDesignTemplates.com

Spirit Guides: 3 Steps To Connecting And Communicating With Your Spirit Helpers/ Blair Robertson. -- 1st ed.

To Granda

"Contact with spirit guides can provide answers to what happens after death, and can also provide help and support for the people left behind when someone dies."

—RICHARD WEBSTER

CONTENTS

Let's Meet Your Spirit Guides!

I'm Blair Robertson, and I thank you so much for purchasing Spirit Guides.

The purpose of this book is to inspire you to have a deeper and more loving, personal relationship with your spirit guide. Yes, you do have a spirit guide. By the end of this book, I intend to not only introduce you to that guide, but to have you interacting, developing, and growing with that guide.

The lessons you will learn come from my live presentations and workshops in which I've literally helped thousands of people experience their guides on a personal level. One of the things I'm known for is being straight to the point; I use very little "woo-woo" language. Unlike a lot of my fellow spiritual advisors and mediums, I like to keep things grounded. I like to be direct and get you to your destination as quickly as possible.

To stay on that course, I'm not including any history of spirit guides or digressing in any way. We're sticking straight to introducing you to the spirit guides and getting you to your destination so that you're interacting with them on a daily basis.

Whether you're a beginner or expert in connecting with your spirit guide, Spirit has shown me principles during the 30 years I've been doing this that enable me to help people of all levels of abilities and skill sets.

One last thing: note that there are a couple of bonuses included with this book. One is an awesome guided meditation. The other is a free webinar I offer from which thousands of people around the world have benefited. Please take a look at them and make them a part of your journey.

Chapter One

Who Are My Spirit Guides?

From the moment you're born and take your first breath until the day you die and breathe your last, your spirit guide is assigned to you every step of the way. Your guide's purpose is to help you live your life to the fullest, achieve the highest karma, and live the richest and happiest life you could possibly attain. That doesn't mean that during your lifetime you won't have challenges, problems, or difficulties. Many of these aspects are put into your lives to grow. We're supposed to have ups and downs, but your guides are there to go for the ride with you.

It's also important to know that while the guides are there for you and want the best for you, you have free will. What does that mean? It means exactly what it says. The word 'guide' is to literally guide you along the way, to give you some direction, to let you know where you should go. But it's up to you – your free will – to make the choice to either do something or not do something. You do not have to listen to what your guides have to say. You do not have to follow their suggestions. You have free given to you by the highest power.

One of the most common questions I'm asked is "How do I know I have a guide?". The answer is actually a fairly simple one. You've probably heard the expression, "Your conscience is your guide." That's it, right there. Your spirit guide uses your conscience to guide you.

When I was a little boy, about seven years old, there was a variety store down the street from my school. I was in there one day, but had no money. That was par for the course since I grew up poor. I saw a pack of gum I wanted, so when nobody was looking, I stole it. And guess what? I got away with it scot-free. Nobody saw me, including the man who owned the shop. But for years, that bothered me. It was only a five-cent pack of gum, but it just kept eating at me and eating at me and eating at me. Even as I went through high school, passing by that variety store, I never stopped in because I felt so horrible about what I'd done a decade earlier. It was a terrible feeling.

Finally, one day after I graduated high school, I was driving past the store and couldn't take it anymore. I hit the brakes, turned around, and went back to it. When I walked in the store, I swear the man standing behind the counter was the man working it when I took the gum. I reached into my pocket and pulled out a $20 bill. I nervously slammed it down on the counter, mumbled that I stole a pack of bubble gum when I was seven years old, told him this was the payback for it – plus interest – then I quickly walked out. The man behind the counter had this blank expression on his face. I don't know if he thought he was being spoofed, or if maybe I was going to rob him – he just stared. But when I drove away, I felt so much better because I cleared my karmic debt. I was no longer a thief of a five-cent pack of gum.

So, what was it that bothered me all of those years? What was it that ate at me? Let me assure you, not a soul saw me steal that pack of gum, including the owner. I got away with it. But my spirit guide knew that I did it and that it wasn't how it was meant to be. My spirit guide rode my back for years until I ended up paying back the man, and I feel so much better today because of it. I corrected a wrong that I made as a silly and stupid child. That's why your guides are there – to give you that direction.

Your conscience is your guide. If you don't believe you have a guide, just follow your conscience – that's what is giving you direction. That's how you can do something in complete secret and have something bother you, whether it be something as silly as stealing a pack of bubble gum, thinking bad thoughts, or something worse.

The cool part of all of this is that you're either allowing your guides to help you or you're blocking them. It's in your control. This goes back to the free will that I was speaking about earlier. You can allow them to help you or you can block them. It really is that simple.

Consider this analogy:

One time I called one of my buddies and left a message, but he didn't call me back. So a week went by and I phoned him again. Same thing...left a message, didn't call back. I waited a few more weeks. Still nothing from him. I tried again. Nothing. About a month later, I saw his father filling up gas at the same gas station I was at. I told him about my attempts to reach his son and asked him to have him call me. He said he would – but I never heard from him

So, what did I do? I did what most people would do—I stopped calling him, and have never heard from him. That's what it's like with your spirit guides. When your spirit guides are assigned to you when you're born, they're there for you. But if you ignore them, they go into the shadows, so to speak, as I did with my buddy. They sort of sit back, relax, they're not hurt, they're not offended. But if you're not actively using your spirit guides, they won't interfere with you; they'll just let you go on your own way.

You have to invite your guides in to have that connection with them. If you want your guides to help you, all you have to do is call upon them – and that's what I'm going to show you how to do.

There are two misconceptions many people have about spirit guides that I want to clear up before going forward.

One is that your spirit guide lived before you did. Your spirit guides have not lived in your time. They were not once part of your family. There are arguments about whether they were ever actually earthbound like us, but that's inconsequential. For the purposes of this conversation, simply know that your guides have not lived before you. That means your grandmother who passed away when you were a child cannot be your guide. Nor can your grandfather or friend. The guides that are assigned to you have been on the other side for a very long time and have chosen to help you. Think of them as spiritual helpers of the highest power, looking after you. Their assignment is to take care of you.

The other misconception is that your guide is supposed to do things for you. That's not true. A lot of people ask their guides, or ask Spirit to do things for them. To ask Spirit to make money appear in a bank account or to change something or fix something is not the purpose of a guide. Your guides do not do things for you. Your guides literally guide you.

Think of it this way: you're driving down a road and you come to a T. You're not sure if you should go to the left or the right. Standing on the corner is an older gentleman, a wise- and friendly-looking man. You roll down your window and shout, "Excuse me, which way should I go, left or right?" The man tells you to go right. You go that way and, lo and behold, you make it to your destination safely. That person standing on the corner is the equivalent to your guide – he gave you good advice with his directions, but that's it. He didn't drive your car, fill it up with gas, or promise you that there wouldn't be some bumps in the road. He gave you the direction, and you followed it. That's the purpose of your spirit guides.

Chapter Two

How to Protect Yourself with White Light

A lot of people worry unnecessarily about evil spirits, or negative things happening to them when they're connecting with their spirit guides. So let's go back to square one. When you were created, you were created from spirit, from the source, from God – from whatever you call the highest power. So, you are a being of light. Your spirit guides were assigned to you by the highest power to help you along your physical path and physical journey. So, when you think of it logically, the very fact that you're from the light and your guides are from the light, there's absolutely nothing to be afraid of. In fact, there's no sane reason why you shouldn't be listening to your guides.

With that said, I've read a number of books and have heard other spiritual leaders discuss darkness and the dangers. Quite frankly, I'm not at all surprised why people are so frightened by that. But let me explain how your guides can help you eliminate that fear.

Picture a very sharp knife. It can be used carefully and safely to cut various foods. But it can also be unwisely used. You could cut yourself, or cut someone else. The knife itself is neither good nor bad. What matters is how you use it. It's the same with your guides. They are inherently safe. It's how you use them that matters. You don't need to fear the darkness. As many religious texts talk about, light always dispels darkness.

If you're in a dark room and can't see anything, you light up a candle or a flashlight or flick on the lights to see. The light immediately destroys the darkness. That's what it's like with us. We don't need to worry about the evil and darkness because we dispel it through the light within us.

With all of that said, it never hurts to protect yourself with white light. It's almost like double protection to ensure that everything is good. Here is how to do that through a quick and simple meditation.

White Light Meditation

Close your eyes and imagine you're in a beautiful field.

There are beautiful rolling hills in every direction.

You're in the middle of nowhere, nobody can bother you, nobody can get to you.

Now just breathe.

Straight above you is the sky, and clouds, and a beautiful white light coming through those clouds and shining down on you like a spotlight.

That bright white light is so bright, so warm. It feels like you're bathing in it, almost like standing in a shower with it flowing over you. It's an incredibly awesome feeling.

But you're not only surrounded in the white light...it flows inside you. It fills up every single molecule of you. You are flooded with that white light.

You can now choose for that white light to remain with you, or you can turn it off. I'm going to ask you to let it remain with you. I want you to say thank you.

There you go. You're filled with white light. That light dispels the darkness.

Connecting with spirit is completely safe. By surrounding and filling yourself with white light, you've got added protection.

The rule of thumb is this: don't play with fire. I jokingly say in my live events to avoid evil like the plague. Don't 'conjure' up evil spirits and you'll be fine.

I had a discussion with a person recently about things like the Ouija board. Is the Ouija board dangerous? If you're walking down a street and you see a portal to hell, don't open it. I usually say that with a big smile in front of my audiences, and it gets a good laugh from them, because who in their right mind would open a portal to hell? But, if you use things like Ouija boards or anything else to conjure up the dark side, then that's your own doing. So, my advice is simple: don't do that. Fill yourself and surround yourself with white light. Connect with your spirit guides, and all shall be well.

Chapter Three

Connecting With Your Guide

I remember when I first learned how to drive a standard car. You put one foot on the brake and the other foot on the clutch before putting the car into first gear and letting the clutch out a little bit. Then you put your foot on the gas, let the clutch out, and drive away. You have to do so many crazy things. When I first started learning how to drive, I thought I would never learn it all. But just a few weeks later, I was whipping down the highway, going up and down the gears, and stopping and starting without any problem. It all flowed together.

That's what I want to do with you here regarding connecting with your guide. I want to break it down into the three basics so that you understand them and can quickly put them together to start enjoying the benefits immediately.

The real key to succeeding with connecting with your spirit guides is to follow your heart, not your mind. The messages that you're going to be getting from your guides are going to be very subtle. Remember, spirit is energy, so there's not a physical person standing beside you that can communicate with you or show you things or tell you things or push you out of the way when there's danger coming along. It's something that's very, very subtle. The more aware you become of it, the better it will be.

I have another tip for you that's extremely important—most people fail because they create expectations. What do I mean by that? It means that this is spiritual, not mechanical. Don't limit your guides. For example, a lot of people will demand that their guides show them a sign. "Show" implies that you're going to see something visual, but your guides may not show you something visual. It might be something that you hear, smell, or feel. It might be something that comes together in a really unique situation outside of expectations that you created.

It's okay to use the expression "show me a sign," but don't limit it to being a visual, something you hear, something you feel, or something that happens at a certain time – such as when you are asleep. It can come anytime, anywhere, and in any manner. Be open to receiving it, and you'll be ready to go.

So, let's talk about what I call the domino effect. One of the things that occurs when you're connecting with your spirit guides is a domino effect – when something happens first that leads to another thing that leads to another thing that ultimately leads to a revelation to you. The effects my come subtly, so something might happen in the morning when you're going to work. Then when you're at work, something else might happen. Then at lunch time, a colleague may say something as part of that effect. Finally, when you're driving home, you hear something on the radio that ultimately gives you the overall message. This is how your spirit guides often work.

A friend of mine was considering moving to another country. He wanted to provide a religious service in another country and he wasn't sure which of the countries he should go to. But, when he was driving along, he heard an interview with a Dutch doctor on some sort of medical procedure (my friend was Dutch and was driving in Ontario). Later on, when reading the newspaper a day or two later, he saw that there was some sort of musician from Holland coming over that his mother really loved. The bottom line is that, after a few of these situations, he realized he needed to go to

Holland. That's where he wanted to go and do his religious outreach.

So, that was the way of his guides underscoring where he needed to go. Interestingly enough, that's not where he initially wanted to go. That's where he felt his guides were really guiding him to go and where he could have the maximum effect.

Be aware of these things because they will all come together for you, and for your higher good. Remember, your spirit guides are here to help you. One of the things I like to tell people is this: try not to overthink. When you overthink things, you suffer from what one of my high school teachers called "paralysis by analysis." Don't be struggling to look for the signs. They will come to you. If you miss the first couple of signs, like my friend did going to Holland (it didn't initially click with him that the radio show and the newspaper ad were the signs), realize that it will eventually all come together. He realized over a couple of days that he was getting the signs that he needed.

That's what you want to do. Don't want to suffer from paralysis by analysis. You want to be open. Don't overthink. It will become very clear to you, if you're open to it.

The next three chapters will explain how to connect with your spirit guides using three easy steps: understanding the five signs of communication, quieting your mind (using any of three different techniques), and interacting for a happier and more fulfilling life.

Chapter Four

Step One: Understanding the Five Signs of Communication

Spirit uses the five senses to communicate with us. You've probably heard a lot of people say that psychics have a sixth sense. That's completely untrue. No psychic has sixth sense. Nobody has a sixth sense. We only have five senses.

You've may have heard of what psychics refer to as "Clairs." Clairvoyant, Clairsentient, etc. Claire is a French word that literally just means "clear." So what our guides will do is use our senses that we already have and heighten them so that we can get better use out of them.

What are the five senses that we have? Seeing, hearing, smelling, tasting and touching.

Your guides will communicate with you using sight by having you see a newspaper or a billboard or something on television. You might see a scenario, or a person that will remind you of something. These are visuals that will bring you to something.

For example, my wife and I have hummingbird feeders outside of our home office. My wife loves hummingbird feeders. Hummingbirds coming around all the time. Just recently, before I sat down to put this book together, a hummingbird came by and flew outside of my window. It reminded me of a hummingbird feeder that my mother used to have outside of her window at a cottage that my parents used to own. That in turn made me think of a conversation that I had with my mother 25 years ago that had a message for me. In other words, the hummingbird brought the memory, which brought the memory of my mother, which brought the memory of the conversation I was having just out of the blue that put it all together for me. That's how it works. It's beautiful.

So, in this particular case, I saw something which started the domino effect of one thing leading to another.

You may also hear something that could trigger a message – a particular sound or noise. But here's the trick: you may hear a real sound, or you may think you're hearing a sound. You could hear something like the sound of a person's voice from the past. It could be something as simple as your first grade teacher who said something. Or, as I just mentioned, my high school teacher who always talked about paralysis by analysis.

Smells can also be signs. It could be walking past flowers, or a scent such a perfume or a cigar.

My Great Uncle Kay smoked a pipe with a custom blend of cherry tobacco. He took quite a shine to me when I was a kid and taught me several cool magic tricks that I used to impress my first grade classmates. He encouraged me to step out of my shell and was very patient with me. While I'm a non-smoker, I can still smell that unique aroma, and it's often when I'm lacking confidence. It's my spirit guides encouraging me.

You can get messages through touching things.

Have you ever held an antique that has taken you back in time, so to speak? While much of this is nostalgic and imagination, there are times when you will touch something of significance and you'll simply 'know' that your guides are giving you a message.

Earlier this year I was thinking of a friend of mine in Australia. I'd been thinking of him on and off for a few days and made a mental note to reply to his last letter.

Days went by and I finally pulled out the letter. Upon touching the letter and uncomfortable feeling came over me. I felt an urgency that is hard to put into words. Rather than write him, I decided to phone him.

I got hold of his wife who had just that morning had my friend admitted to hospital and would soon be diagnosed with pancreatic cancer, and died not long after.

It was the touch of the letter and the energy contained that my guides used to alert me that something was wrong.

Had I had written him back—or emailed him—I wouldn't have had a last chance to chat to him, which I got, thanks to my spirit guides.

Tasting is another way to receive signs.

Not as common as the other forms of signs, you can often get messages from taste as well. My mother was a wonderful woman but a horrendous cook. She made the world's most bland food. But every so often when I taste bland food—or simply think of it—there is a message of something that she taught me. I consider this to be an indirect way of communicating, yet still powerful.

The bottom line is this: be open to everything. It could be a song on the radio or a television show. It could be words on a page. It could be something like a scent of a cigar or perfume of some sort. It could be a bumper sticker or one of those vanity plates on a car. It could be anything. Just be open to the signs and let the signs flow. Don't judge them. They—the spirit guides – will create ways for you to piece the puzzle together.

Let's do a quick recap. You may see something this morning at work and it won't have any impact on you. Somebody might say something to you in the middle of the day at work or at lunch time, or something might happen – suddenly, all of the pieces will start to come together. You will get that "ah-ha" moment. That is one of the main ways that your spirit guides will communicate with you.

There is one more thing that I need to teach you, and it's outside of the five signs: your guides are able to connect with you while you're sleeping. So, there's a difference between sleeping and having dreams. When you have a dream, a dream is typically really unusual or weird. The example I like to give is an actual dream that I had one time. I imagined or dreamt that I got out of bed—I had to go to work and I jumped on a big giant rubber ducky and I floated down a stream which was in place of my street. Of course, you wake up and you think, "Wow, what was that all about?"

Here's the thing to remember: dreams are usually weird and often nonsensical. You'll see people in dreams, like a postman, but one of the signs that you're dreaming is that you usually can't describe the person. You know it's the postman, you know it's a male, but you can't remember their face when you wake up. That's how dreams work. They're not scary people when you see them, they're just sort of blank. You just know the role they're in or who they are or what they are, but typically you're not able to see them. However, while you're sleeping, before you're dreaming, is usually when the connections will come through.

The connections are going to be very, very strong. The connections are going to be very, very clear. You will see things and know things, and everything will be extremely clear to you in such a way that there will be no doubt what it is. That's how your guides can make a connection with you and bring messages to you. It will all be very, very clear.

The messages from our guides will often be so clear that we will know we have to move or have to make a phone call or do something else. In many, many ways, they're able to communicate with us. It will be a message delivered and message received. You will know it when you wake up – if you're aware of it.

Now that you know the five signs of communication and are open to them, let's move to the next step: Quieting Your Mind.

Chapter Five

Step Two: Quieting Your Mind

"Life is available only in the present moment" –
Thich Nhat Hahn

We live in a crazy, busy world, wouldn't you agree? My wife and I recently went out to have a nice dinner and decided to treat ourselves, so we went to what you would call an upper-scale steakhouse. We played the part. We dressed up nice and we were really looking forward to it.

When we were there, at the place across from us was a slightly older couple. I thought, "Oh isn't that nice, another gentleman taking his lovely wife out." But for the entire dinner, both of them were on their cell phones texting, communicating, and surfing. They weren't even talking to each other. That goes back to what Thich Nhat Hahn said: "Life is available only in the present moment."

There they were, at a beautiful steakhouse (which was not cheap), and instead of spending some quality time with each other, they were keeping up with the outside world and missing out on a beautiful dinner and a beautiful opportunity to really connect.

It's amazing to see how many people live such crazy, busy lives. I have a client that I recently spoke to who was complaining about how stressed he was. When he started listing all of the things that were on his plate, it was incredible. He literally had so many responsibilities that he was probably doing the jobs of three to four people. It was insane. It's no wonder he was stressed out. But here's the sad part: he was unwilling to do anything about it.

There's a great story from Zen that I learned as a young teenager. It's called "Empty Your Cup," and goes like this:

Many, many years ago, there was a young man who became quite proficient in sword fighting in Japan. He was winning awards and becoming renowned around the area. All of his teachers ran out of new things that they could teach him, so they told him that the only person who could teach him now was this man at the top of a mountain, a real Zen master. He was an old man who was once one of the greatest sword fighters on the planet.

The student is smart enough to realize that's a good idea. So he makes the journey up this mountain to meet this man, and the man invites him in. They shuffle to the table where they both kneel down. In Japanese tradition, the old man starts to make tea. He places two cups out and starts to make the tea while the young man starts to regale him with all of the stories of how wonderful and great he is, all of the techniques he's used, and all of the people that he's beaten. He keeps talking and talking while the old man patiently and quietly listens as he makes the tea.

The young man continues bragging and talking and discussing all the things he knows as the old man starts to pour the tea into his cup. It's a tradition to pour for the guest before you pour for yourself, so he starts to fill up the young man's tiny cup. As the cup fills up, it starts to overflow while the old man smiles and keeps nodding at the young man, who keeps on bragging and talking about all of his great skills. The young man notices the tea overflowing, but thinks perhaps the old man is a little senile and just allows it to happen.

The tea continues to pour out of the glass onto the table top, eventually reaching the edge and dropping over the side, burning the young man's legs. The young man jumps up and yells, "Are you crazy old man? Can't you see this cup is full?" The old man raises his hand, smiles, and gestures for the young man to sit back down. As the old man puts down the teapot, he says to the young man, "This is your mind. Your mind is so full, just like this cup. You have no way of learning anything new. For you to move forward in life, you must first empty your cup, then you'll be ready to receive."

That's what it's like here in the world today. We need to learn how to quiet our minds. We need to center ourselves. We need to take time for ourselves so that we can become aware of spirit. We're often so busy that there's no way for spirit to be able to make a connection with us. So, the best way to do it is to learn how to relax your mind, center yourself. When you center yourself, you become one with spirit.

I'm going to teach you three techniques you can use to do just that. I want you to use them three times a day to get started. Do it once in the morning, once at noon, and once at nighttime. Of course, if you want to do it more, by all means, do it. Here's the really cool part: most of the techniques I'm about to teach you – nobody is going to know you're doing them because you're not going to be chanting. You're not going to be singing. You're not going to have to strip naked and lay underneath the moonlight. It's all stuff that you can do anytime, anywhere, any place, and it only takes a moment or two to do. Once you start learning to quiet your mind, you will open your reception to Spirit to make connections.

I do want to make one thing clear: Spirit may use this opportunity to show you something, or may use this opportunity while you're meditating, to remind you of all of the things you've been missing because you've been busy for the past few hours. But, either way, it will clear your mind, allow you to be more receptive and, if you can master this, it will only help and improve your life.

So, let's begin.

Technique 1: Following Your Breath.

This one is my favorite, and one that I use on a daily basis. You don't need anything to do this. What I want you to do is breathe for a few moments. Breathe in through your nose and out through your mouth. It's as simple as that.

Unlike a lot of other meditative techniques that teach you to breathe in deeply and hold it, and then let it out with a sigh, you will not be doing that. You're just simply going to breathe, something that you've been doing since you were first born.

Imagine you can see your breath, like when it's cold outside. You can see it floating. Now imagine that you can see your breath going in through your nose, filling up your lungs, and exiting your mouth. See the breath go out.

This technique is called "Following Your Breath" because you are literally going to watch the breath go in through your nose. I want you to imagine you can see it filling your lungs up, and then when you naturally need to exhale, you just breathe it back out again.

Now imagine that you're sitting with other people. If the person beside you was just running, they're going to be breathing very, very quickly. You don't need to keep up with them. If you're breathing quickly, you don't have to focus on slowing your breath, you just have to concentration on breathing. Your body will naturally regulate it to the perfect state you need to be in. If the person beside you was breathing very, very slowly, you don't have to match his or her speed. Everyone has a unique pace of breathing in and out. Your job is simply to follow your breath.

You can do this with your eyes open, though I like to do this with my eyes closed. I would also like to point out that, if you were on a public bus or train going to work, for example, you could be sitting beside somebody and doing this meditation without that person even knowing what you're doing. There's no signs that you're actually doing the meditation; it's very cool.

As you do this breathing technique, you'll notice at some point that it will feel like a light is surrounding you and melting off the negative energies. It will feel like it's melting off the stresses. It will feel like it's burning away the things that are troubling you. You don't even need to think about that, it will just happen automatically for you.

What's also really cool about this technique is that you just follow your breath. If your mind is really busy and you're thinking of all kinds of other things, stuff that you have to do – maybe you have to pick up some groceries after work – don't let it distract you. Just acknowledge it and continue to follow your breath. You're not ignoring those other thoughts, you're just concentrating on your breath right now.

After about two minutes, you can stop and you'll discover that you'll feel much, much better. That's because you've only been focusing on your breath, which helps you naturally hit your base rhythm, which will allow you to connect with spirit. You will be centering yourself. It happens very quickly, and it only takes about two minutes to do. I use this one on a regular basis. It works tremendously well and is by far my favorite because you don't need to be anywhere special. You don't need to do anything unique. I use it multiple times a day, probably 10-15 times, maybe more. It's something that is easily used and easily acceptable.

Technique 2: Tick Tock Method

This second technique was created by a very good friend of mine, Richard Webster. He's written more than 125 books on psychic topics. He calls this the "Tick Tock Method." This is a little variation on what he taught and it works very well. For this one, it's best for you to close your eyes. When you close your eyes, you're going to imagine a big clock. Go back in your memory and find a large white clock with the black numbers and the black hands. For some of you, it might be the giant clock you had in school. Maybe it's a clock at the library, or the main one in your home town. It doesn't make a difference. Just mentally see a giant, white clock with the black numbers and the black hands.

With your eyes closed, you're going to hear the clock making the tick, tock, tick, tock" sound. Imagine that you can hear it. Hear it in your mind. Now I want you to watch the little red hand that's slowly making itself around in circles, around the clock. As you're watching the clock, I want you to see the numbers slowly either melt away or slowly drop off. As the numbers start to drop off from 1 to 12, you'll notice that you're starting to feel much more relaxed. The numbers are just dropping one at a time. The clock is slowly becoming a blank clock with only the hands moving around.

Just keep that tick tock sound going in your mind. You're just watching the clock with fascination. Then, notice how the hands on the clock drop away. Right at this point, you're now looking at a white circle, and you'll notice how relaxed you are. Then, open up your eyes and you will be centered again. It's such an easy technique to use. It sounds more complicated than it really is. Just watch the numbers and the hands disappear, and for some weird and strange reason that I don't even pretend to understand, it just happens to relax you. I believe it makes you more aware of time. I believe it makes you value the time. This is the time for yourself, so you get to enjoy it and recognize that as time marches on, this is your time – and the time to connect with Spirit.

Technique 3: Mental Vacation

This third technique is also a simple one. Go back in your mind and find a place where you have gone, perhaps even taken a vacation to that was perhaps, up until this point, one of the most ultimate experiences. It should be a place where you found complete and total peace.

The memory that works best for me was from many years ago. I was in my early 20s and I got to take a vacation down to the Dominican Republic. I remember standing with my feet in the ocean up to about my knees. The water was so warm. I could feel the warm breeze blowing, and I could smell the salt of the water. I could feel the waves hitting my knees and the sand beneath my toes. I was just thinking at that moment that I was in paradise. It was the middle of winter and a far cry from the snow banks six feet deep where I was living back in Canada.

It was such a peaceful experience and was so embedded in my mind that I can still think of that right now and get that same warm, awesome feeling. You take literally a mental vacation. It doesn't matter what the mental vacation is, but you want to meditate on it. That's the key word – meditate. Do it for one to two minutes. Enjoy that awesome, peaceful feeling that you had at this location.

I have a relative that likes to climb mountains. When he gets to the top of the mountain, he takes incredible photos in which you can see as far as the eye can see. To him, that's the ultimate in relaxation. Even though it was physically draining, it's a sense of triumph. For other people it might be something much different. It could be somewhere cold, somewhere old, somewhere isolated. Whatever you consider paradise to be, go there in your mind.

As you immerse yourself in that place, use all five of your sense to enjoy it. What do you see? What do you hear? What do you feel? What do you smell? What do you taste?

Doing this for two minutes literally clears out all of the distractions, all of the noise, and returns you back to being centered. It returns you back to being you and allows you to find that inner peace once again. It really works.

Now, before I forget, please, for free, you can get my guided meditation. I have a meditation MP3 recording for you that you can download free of charge, as the owner of this book. You can go to it. There is nothing—there's no trick to it, there's nothing to buy. You just download it and use it. It will help you with any of these three techniques. So, please make sure you go to this link, download it and use it. It will help you. I will also review all three techniques.

The secret isn't which technique is better. I love the first one – Follow Your Breath. That's the one that works best for me. Or maybe you'll prefer the Tick Tock Method. Or the Mental Vacation. It makes no difference which one you use. I prefer the first one because nobody knows you're doing it when you're following your breath. You can use it anywhere, anytime. You don't need music for it. You don't need to listen to anything. You just do it.

If you can do one or more of these techniques at least three times a day, you're only going to benefit from them. Your life is going to be much more peaceful. Your guides are going to be able to access you and give you the information that you're looking for, which will help you to live your life to the fullest. You will feel more aware, and you will feel much more spiritual. How much better can that be?

Chapter Six

Step Three: How to Interact for a Happier and More Fulfilling Life

Let's do a quick recap. You've now learned the five different ways of communication with your guides – seeing, hearing, smelling, tasting, and touching. You have also learned three techniques – Following Your Breath, the Tick Tock Method, and the Mental Vacation – for quieting your mind. This should all eventually become second nature to you, like riding a bike. You won't even think about it.

Now we're going to move on to what I call the Gold, which is interacting with our guides for a happier and more fulfilled life.

How can I guarantee success and instantly improve communications with my guides?

Has anyone ever asked you for advice in which you gave it, but they either didn't follow it or just completely ignored it? Isn't that frustrating? Doesn't that make you just want to choke the person? I'm kidding of course, but how do you think Spirit reacts when you ask for guidance, direction, and then you don't follow those instructions? It's insulting and rude to Spirit because Spirit comes from the highest power. Spirit's goal is to help give you the direction and guidance that you need. It may not be the guidance and direction that you want, but it will always be the guidance and direction that will give you the most fulfilling life possible. Your spirit guides are not designed to ensure that you never have roadblocks or bumps in the road. They're there to help you learn lessons along the way, but to learn them in the fastest and quickest ways possible.

What's the best way to appreciate and value your spirit's guidance? What do you do with the information that you get? Here's the secret: you take action on it. Because anything less than taking action on the guidance that your guides give you is completely and totally disrespectful. Again, you don't have to like the information, but it's important that you take action.

I'm not a doctor, but if I were and I recognized that you needed to have your foot amputated, I wouldn't expect you to be happy to hear it. Also, as a doctor, I wouldn't be happy to tell you that you need your foot amputated. But here's the deal: it has to be brought up, and it has to be addressed, because that's what's ultimately in your best interests. Again, you don't have to like the guidance, but following the guidance will likely help you in the best manner possible.

Your guides have a role. They're there to literally guide you. But you must learn the life lessons. For example, I have a friend who is a fitness instructor. She always points out a very funny expression that always makes me laugh. She says, "I can't do your push-ups for you." In other words, she can show you how to do the proper exercises, she can teach you the proper form, she can teach you everything you need to know about doing them, but ultimately it's you who has to drop to the floor and start doing those push-ups so that you can enjoy the benefits. Just like learning to read or write, we can show you the things that you need to do, but it's ultimately you that has to put the eyes to the page or pen to the paper.

So remember, the way that you can guarantee success with your communications with your guides is this: take action on what they show you, and learn from the lessons that they experience along the way. Remember that your guides are going to give you help at exactly the right time and in exactly the right place.

How to Set Intentions

What's the difference between asking your guides questions and intentions? Most people make the mistake of asking their guides open-ended, indefinite, or unspecific questions. The secret to having success with your guides is to set an intention.

A question might be something as silly as, "Gosh guides, do you think that I can really lose weight?" It's a very vague question that does not give a definitive goal that you want to achieve, or a plan to achieve it.

However, an intention is when you set a specific goal of something that you want to be, do, or have. It's something that you want to achieve and that you need help with. For example, if you're a person who tends to overeat or overindulge, you can set an intention with your guides that you intend to stop doing that, that you intend to lose 20 pounds in the next 60 days, and that you are requesting your guide's to help you achieve that specific goal.

This is a huge difference. What this does is give your guides specifics that they can support you with. They can jump in and help you and let you know that your plate is too large if you're trying to lose that amount of weight, or that you're eating the wrong foods, or that you're eating too often, or that you're not following the guidelines. It's an intention that they're able to get on board with and help you with. They will help you design and achieve the life that you want. If you tend to be terrible at handling your finances, don't say to your spirit guides, "I'm terrible at my finances; help me!" There's nothing they can do with that, but if you intend to start budgeting and live within your budget, you can ask them to help you with the willpower to follow the specific budget guidelines that you've laid out for yourself so you can live within your means.

What will my guides do for me?

The simple answer to that question is this—your guides are going to help you in any single possible way, whether that's once a day or a hundred times a day, to achieve those specific intentions. They're there to help you.

Look back in time when Thomas Edison had it in his mind that he was going to invent a light bulb. The concept of the light bulb, as I understand it, was pretty basic. The problem was getting a filament that could heat up, cool down, and then heat up again without disintegrating. He could create a light that could work one time, but that was it. Thomas Edison invented that in the early days, but he needed something better. He knew that there must be something on this planet that could withstand that kind of heat variable.

He set in his mind to find it. He created that intention. I'm sure, from what we know, that he must've had days where he was terribly frustrated. In fact, as the story goes, he tried 10,000 different types of materials to try to discover what would work. I can't imagine trying just 10 things myself, can you? I would've given up long before that, but his intention was to find it, and find it he did. To this very day, we still have those incandescent light bulbs he invented so long ago because he set that intention. His guides, I'm utterly convinced—utterly convinced – helped him along the way to discover what was necessary to create that incandescent light bulb.

Here are a couple of tips to help you set your intentions:

•   When you set an intention, keep it as simple as possible. I'm a big believer in brainstorming. Take a piece of paper and sketch out what you want to accomplish and where you need the help. It really is that simple. Don't say, "I want to lose weight." Come up with a specific weight amount that you need to lose, come up with a specific plan to achieve that, and then ask your guides to help you with those goals.

• If there's something that you want to accomplish—such as saving money for the down payment of a house – set a specific intention and ask your guides to help create two things for you: the energy to stick to your plan, and other ways you can create income that will help you get to your goal faster. Your guides will then start taking action for you.

It really is that simple. And, remember, the intentions and the interactions that they're going to have with you are going to be their timing, not yours. So don't set an intention tonight and expect to have all of the answers tomorrow. All of the answers tomorrow may not be available. You may have to take the first step, the second step, and the third step before your guides will meet you at the altar, so to speak.

This reminds me of an old joke:

There's a guy who lives beside a very wealthy man. They're about the same age, just out of high school. All of a sudden this guy gets a big fancy car, one that's really expensive. The guy climbs to the top of this hill and prays, "God, why not me?, Why not me?, How come I don't get the car? I'm so good, I do everything for you...Why not me, God?" He goes back home angry and frustrated. A few days later, the next door neighbor with the fancy car gets himself an absolutely drop-dead gorgeous model of a girlfriend. So the guy goes back up to the top of the hill and he complains some more: "Why not me, God? Why? Why? I do everything for you. I'm a nice guy. And he gets a car and he gets a beautiful girl!".

This goes on and on and on for days and days and days. He then goes up to the top of the hill to complain some more about something else that the other guy has that he doesn't have. That's when the clouds open up, the earth shakes and shutters, and from the heavens comes the booming voice of God who finally answers his question: "Because you bug me."

This might not be the funniest joke in the world, but it's humorous in the sense that so often we pray for things and we ask and we beg and we continue to repeat our desires over and over and over again. With Spirit, you only need to ask for what you want one time. Do not make the mistake of asking repeatedly. You do not have to pray 10, 15 or 20 times a day. You don't have to pray the same prayer every day for a month. Spirit knows what you're looking for. Spirit guides want to help you achieve what you're looking to achieve in life.

All you need to do is simply set your intention, then leave the rest to your spirit guides and Spirit. It is better, instead of praying, to actually start taking action. Ask for what you need, ask for the help and the guidance that you're looking for, and then get on that path and start moving.

There's an expression that I love that I repeat to myself all the time: motion beats meditation. Instead of thinking and dreaming and dreaming and thinking, it's better to take action on the things that you want to achieve in your life. That's all you need to do. Say what you need, set your intention, and then start taking action.

When is the best time to set the intention for the ultimate response? I have discovered, from having done this for 30 years, that the best time to set your intention is late at night, just before you're about to go to sleep. Whatever it is that you've decided you would like to ask Spirit to do, do whatever it is you need to do and then, when you get into bed, pull the covers up, roll over, and simply do your breathing exercise. Breathe in and breathe out. Become one with Spirit. Then simply ask, as clearly as possible, what you would like the help with. Once you have passed that on to Spirit, know that Spirit has it. Then close your eyes and simply go to sleep.

While you're sleeping, Spirit and spirit guides will take that information and begin formulating a process to make these happen. You do not need to repeat them 100 times. You don't have to beg, you don't have to plead; just simply state what it is you would like to achieve, what you need the help with, and then simply go to sleep.

I want to share with you one amazing technique that you can use tonight to make a connection with your guides—I call it my Rapid Start Technique.

I want you to go to bed tonight and do the breathing meditation that I shared. Please make sure that you download the free MP3 mediation that I have included with this book. The one thing I want you to ask your spirit guides is this simple, easy question: what is the one thing I can do tomorrow to improve my karma?

If you're ever stuck not knowing what to do, not knowing what to ask, or if you're feeling frustrated, challenged, or overwhelmed, simply ask your spirit guides what you can do tomorrow to improve your karma. Then, close your eyes and go to sleep. Your spirit guides will start connecting with you while you're sleeping. Tomorrow morning when you wake up, I don't know what it will be that your guides will show you, but they will show you one thing that's very personal. Maybe you need to make a phone call. Maybe you need to address something. Maybe you need to respond to something. Maybe you need to take action. Maybe you need to set a goal. I don't know what it will be, but you will wake up with an overwhelming compulsion to do something.

I'm not promising you that it will be easy. You may have to confront somebody who has been a big challenge to you by causing you a lot of stress or grief. Maybe you have to call a creditor who's been hounding you. Maybe you need to speak to a lawyer. Maybe you need to address a personal relationship. Maybe you need to ask your boss for a pay raise. Whatever it is, promise yourself that whatever your guides show you, you will take action on it. The benefits will be far greater than the price you paid for this book. This simple technique could literally change your life for the better forever.

Let's face it – some of us have so many challenges on our plates that it seems like we're never going to see the light of day. But we can't change everything overnight. You can, however, change and work on one thing at a time each day and make progress. Remember, there are 365 days in a year. If your guides were to show you 365 things and you were to take action on just one thing a day, imagine how much better your life would be a year from now. Imagine how much better you would feel and how your prospects would dramatically change...all from doing that one simple thing.

The Japanese call it Kaizen, which loosely translates to "constant and never-ending improvement." One of the philosophies the Japanese have that I love so much is that they build something awesome, then they try to make it even more awesome. Using that Kaizen philosophy, what if you did that for your own life? What if every day you did one tiny little thing to improve your life? Imagine all the people you would impact – your spouse, children, family members, coworkers – because you are shining like the bright light that Spirit wants you to be. Your life can change for the better.

As a first step, after reading this book tonight, do your breathing meditation. Just before you go to sleep, ask Spirit what the one thing is that you can do tomorrow to improve your karma. Then promise yourself that no matter how easy or challenging it may seem, you will take action tomorrow morning. That is when you will be setting in motion what you need to do to improve your life.

Your Ultimate Happiness: Manifesting the Life of your Dreams with your Guides

Technically, you now have everything you need to experience more and gain more from life with your spirit guides. But why stop here? Let's explore how you can live the life of your dreams. We were not put on earth just to pass or mark time. We were put here to live our lives to the absolutely fullest. As my late friend, Joe Marino, used to say, "We're here to be more, do more and, yes, have more."

Think about it for a second. If we were made in God's image, as I and many people believe, can we not expect that we're meant to live life to the fullest? Why would you waste the time that you have here? We're only here on earth for a very short amount of time. Make the most of it!

Here's another question for you: why settle for anything less? So many people feel that you have to live like a pauper, but I once heard that there's no virtue in being poor. If that's how you choose to live your life, that's fine, but understand that it's a choice. I'm not implying that you need to become a multi-millionaire in order to be happy. Far from it. Actually, what I am saying is that you should not set your goals too low, or set the bar too low. Aim high. Go big or go home, as they say.

When I do live events and when I teach how to connect with spirit guides, people find it weird that I talk about setting goals. They'll say things to me like, "Well I already know everything about setting goals and that doesn't sound like it's spiritually connected." Oh, how contraire. Setting goals is part of the spiritual experience.

If you're designed to really push past your limitations and live your life to the fullest, the best and fastest way for you to do this is to set high goals for yourself – demanding ones. You have probably heard the story of a guy named Roger Bannister who was the first person to break the four-minute mile. The only reason he broke the four-minute mile is because he set that as a goal for himself and pushed himself to achieve it. Until that time, doctors told him his heart would explode if he ran that fast, but the year he broke the four-minute mile, literally within a couple of years, everyone started breaking it because they understood that if he could do it, so could somebody else. He set a new goal for us.

The sad part of all this is that most people are just drifting through life. They get up in the morning when the alarm clock goes off. They shower and go to work. A lot of people are going to jobs they greatly dislike and, because of that, it negatively affects them emotionally, mentally and, yes, spiritually. So you slog through your day and you go home and because you're mentally and physically and spiritually exhausted, there's little else you can do except maybe have something to eat, watch some television, or surf the Internet, then go to bed and repeat the same thing the next day. That's not how Spirit wants us to live. Spirit wants us to live in the largest, biggest, most fulfilling way we possibly can.

So, the number one tip that I can share with you right now is to define happiness and go for it. Seek it out. One of the quickest fixes that I have known in my 30 years of consulting with people as a psychic and a medium is to get you to ask yourself what makes you happy. This is a very quick fix and it works very well. Think in terms of hobbies. What do you really, really enjoy? Most people – when they're down and negative and drifting through life – give up everything, including a worthwhile hobby. It's a weird thing.

I love blues music and I like playing guitar, particularly blues guitar. I don't expect you to like that, but it's something that I love. I can literally sit down with my guitar and play for hours. I can sit and listen to music in my backyard for hours. The old-time blues music brings me peace and joy and costs almost nothing. My wife, Wendy, loves hummingbirds. We have hummingbird feeders all around our house. She tends to them, looks after the little hummers, and they have a great time.

My wife also loves her garden. I've got a black thumb and have absolutely zero interest in looking after plants, but she gets tremendous joy from it. It costs her next to nothing to do it. Another friend of mine, Geoff, is a boxing fanatic. It's completely outside of the scope of the business he's in. He attends boxing, participates in a lot of events and fundraisers, helps the local community boxers out, and is on a first name basis with many of the greatest living boxing legends. It's something that he absolutely loves and adores.

Start where you are. One of the fastest ways to overcome unhappiness is to get into a hobby or renew a hobby that brings you tremendous joy. Back in the old days they used to call these hobbies "pastimes." It comes from the French word, passe-temps, which literally means "pass time." More accurately, it means to pass time in an enjoyable manner.

Think back to the late 1800s when people would work on a farm all day. Darkness would then fall and they'd have to come in. What was there to do? Nothing. So, they would sing or make quilts or whatever, but what they did was create pastimes that they could enjoy while they were waiting for bed. It was also a very great way of building the family community.

Many years ago I did a very popular motivational seminar for high schools and college conferences. One of the things I did during that seminar was a hypnosis show called "Blair's Ultimate Three-Step Goal Setting Method." At the bottom of the page were three numbers for people to fill it in – the three-step goal setting method. Those three steps were:

1. Set a goal and a reasonable deadline.
2. Write the steps you need to accomplish that goal.
3. Do everything you outlined in Step 2.

Of course, this would get a big laugh because people wouldn't believe it was as simple as that. After all, there were trainers and courses available that would teach you, over a three- and five-day period, how to set goals. But really, when it comes down to it, those are the only three things you need to do to achieve any goal that you wish in life.

Again, goal setting does not need to be hard, nor does it need to be something that's outside the realm of spirituality. In fact, to achieve what you want to do, you should have goals so that when you wake up in the morning, you have something to look forward to. It should be something that gives you drive, a sense of achievement, success, and something to measure yourself against. It should create inspiration. It will give your guides something to work with—like a blank canvas for a painter that they can help you fill in.

Your guides can and will help you achieve your goals. But, you must give your guides something to work with.

I personally like to use the word "intentions" instead of "goals," but they are the same thing. If you don't have a goal, if you don't have an intention, and there's nothing for your guides to help you with. A famous motivational speaker named Zig Ziglar once said, "You can't hit a target that you can't see." He went on to explain the story of a famous archer who used to be able to shoot an arrow, hit the bulls-eye, shoot another arrow, and split the first arrow into two. Ziglar went on to say that he could beat this guy any day of the year, but with one condition: that he would blind fold this man and spin him around a bunch of times. Ziglar's point was driven home by saying, "Of course you would win every time against that guy; how can the archer hit a target he can't see?"

Set goals. Create something to measure against. Create something that inspires you and drives you forward. It may be something small, something tiny. Then you can start building up. Once you've achieve that goal, set another goal and another goal and another goal. There are no limits to the amount of goals you can have.

A friend of mine, Joy, once went from 140 pounds to nearly 250 pounds. This was when we were in high school. It happened so quickly that you could see her getting heavier and heavier every day. I asked her one day what was going on. She said she didn't know. She wasn't eating any more than she used to. She admitted that she drank a lot of pop, and definitely had some pizza and stuff like that, but she was ballooning way out of proportion.

I asked her if she had seen a doctor. She said she hated doctors – didn't trust them. My guides inside me were telling me that I had to somehow urge her into seeing one. I said, "You know, if you keep going the way you're going, you're going to get larger and larger, and it's not going to be good for your health, especially your heart." To make a long story short, she went to her doctor. She expected him to tell her to cut way back on food and start eating like a rabbit. But instead, after a simple little blood test, they discovered the weight gain had something to do with her thyroid. She was given medication, which controlled her thyroid, and she went right back to her previous weight. She looked stunning after the weight quickly dropped off. You see, she wasn't listening to her guides. She wasn't listening to her conscience. She was letting fear get in her way. I truly believe that she could've died from that had she not done something about it.

Another friend of mine, Nancy, also needed to lose weight. She went to her doctor, who gave her the okay to start losing it. She ate better and worked out vigorously, taking karate and lifting weights. Six months later, after taking action, she started getting requests to take pictures for modeling. It was astonishing, but she credited her guides with helping her. Her guides would give her kicks in the butt. When she didn't feel like going to karate, she would still go to karate. They would urge her, they would push her. When she felt like eating really crappy food, her guides would encourage her to keep focused on her end game, and she dropped the weight seemingly easily…but it was a lot of hard work.

She was able to do it because her guides were there for her – and she listened to them.

Another area in which we need to set goals is with money. A lot of people are afraid to set financial goals. A lot of religions teach us to not seek money, that it is the root of all evil. But that's not true. The love of money is the root of evil, not money itself. Greed will do more damage to you than anything else.

My friend, Stewart, was renting a condominium in downtown Toronto. He was paying thousands of dollars a month for it. I was speaking to him one day and I said, "Have you ever looked at buying a house?" He said, "Blair, there's no way I could afford a house in Toronto. It's way too expensive here." He's a very spiritual guy, so I asked him what his guides were saying. "Oh, it just doesn't make any financial sense and I don't feel I deserve it," he said. "I'm just going to keep going the way I'm going."

But with a little bit of encouragement, we discovered that he was completely oblivious to his financial situation. I'm not a financial advisor, but it came quick to me that if he could afford a couple of thousand dollars a month for a condominium, which he didn't own, he could easily turn that into a mortgage payment. To make a long story short, we got online, went to a banking site, and discovered that not only could he afford a home, but he was only a couple of thousand dollars away from a down payment needed to buy himself the house of his dreams. He shook his head and said to me, "Blair, I've been thinking for years that I couldn't afford this, and I have been ignoring the inklings from Spirit because I didn't want to be rejected or told I couldn't afford it." He allowed fear to overcome what his guides were trying to direct him to do. Again, to make a long story short, six months later, he was living in a big house just outside of Toronto, and paying less than what he was paying for the condominium – all because he finally listened to his spirit guides and what Spirit wanted for him.

Stewart wasn't being selfish. He has two small children and a wife and he really wanted the best for them. But now, instead of renting and not getting anything for it, he is now the owner of real estate, his own home, and he's building his equity, which is helping his family and their future.

Goal setting does not need to be tough. Again, there are so many courses out there that spend hours and hours on the subject. Numerous books have been written on how to set goals. But just follow the simple rules:

Number 1: give a reasonable deadline. If you're 200 pounds overweight, don't expect to drop the 200 pounds in 30 days. Get help if you need to. Get some advice.

Check it out with an expert. But set yourself a goal and a reasonable deadline.

Number 2: write the steps you need to accomplish this goal. It may be one or two steps. It may be five or ten steps. But place them in the logical order that they need to be in.

Number 3: do the steps. Do everything in Number 2. Follow the steps – one step at a time.

Lose a couple of pounds a week. Put a few dollars aside for that investment. Do what it takes to get to your goals. After all, nobody deserves it more than you. And if you're looking for permission to succeed, or if you're looking for permission to be, do, or have more—let me help you.

I, Blair Robertson, give you permission to do so.

Ten Most Asked Questions About Spirit Guides (Q&A format)

Are our guides the same as our guardian angels?

That goes a little bit outside the scope of this book, as this book is focused mostly on spirit guides. But, let's just briefly address it in this manner: your spirit guides are assigned to you from birth. Their only job and only responsibility is to personally guide you throughout your lifetime. They're only concerned with you and they're only thought is your personal well-being.

Guardian angels are higher up in the hierarchy. If we imagine the spirit world to be like the Christian form of heaven with God, then God has the guardian angels. The guardian angels, in turn, look after multiple people. It can be groups of people, and very large ones. So their job is more of a general oversight of a group of people, whereas your spirit guides look after you specifically and individually. There's nothing wrong with praying to guardian angels. Guardian angels do exist. They are there to help us as well, but the best thing you can do is focus on your personal spirit guides. They're the ones that have your highest interests at hand.

Do guides only talk to you when you meditate?

No, they can communicate to you any time, any place, and anywhere using any of your five senses. They can show us all kinds of signs and messages at any point in time. The purpose of meditating is so that we can consciously be making those connections and consciously opening ourselves to become one with spirit. It certainly doesn't hurt to pray and meditate because it opens up the channel for your spirit guides to communicate with you better. But you can have them make connections with you at any time. You can be in the middle of a meeting at work and you'll have a sense of something, and it could be through any of the five senses. You'll feel it, you'll experience it, and then know that you need to take action on something. It can happen as quickly as that. So be open and aware to any message that can come through to you at any time during the day, or while you're sleeping at night.

Can they see us all the time, like when I'm having sex?

I get asked this question a lot, and it concerns a lot of people. The good news is that your spirit guides are with you 24/7. They're with you all the time. So, truthfully, yes, while you're in the shower or if you're having sex, yes, they are there with you. But your guides are spiritual, so they have no physical connection, meaning sex to them is meaningless. Your spirit guides don't have sex. They don't eat. They don't sleep. They are not at all concerned with the physical realm. They're concerned specifically with your spiritual well-being. Always remember that you are a spiritual person having a physical experience.

In other words, we're here on this physical plane to learn things, but we are spiritual people within physical bodies. We're not physical people having spiritual experiences; there's a big difference. We're spiritual people having physical experiences – that's the major distinction. So don't worry. Go about your day as always.

Can someone we know be a guide when they cross over?

A lady recently told me that her son had passed away last year and she really believed he was her personal spirit guide. Unfortunately, that is not true. The easiest way to remember these things is with this a saying that I coined: our guides guide us and our loved ones love us. It's just like if your father was here today and you were at work having a challenge. Well, you're a grownup now and if you're having a challenge at work, your dad can't come in like he maybe did at school and talk to the principal about it. If he were alive he would still love and support and encourage you, but you would have to navigate through the work challenge on your own.

It's the same with our guides. Our guides are connected directly to us; they're with us for the ride. Our loved ones, when they crossover to the other side, are there to evolve and to watch us from a distance, but they will not be our spirit guides. It's very important that we make this distinction because it will help us to have richer and fuller lives. When you realize that your guide is only interested in helping you succeed and achieve things in life, that frees you up to still have that knowledge and awareness that your loved ones are safely and comfortably on the other side, but free from having to deal with the physical things here anymore. They're free. They're absolutely free.

That's a good thing and not a bad thing. In this particular lady's case, she took that to mean that her son didn't love her anymore, which I had to clearly point out was simply not true. Although it's tragic that her son passed away, her son is happy and free from all pain on the other side. He still loves her very, very much, but the guides are responsible for guiding her through her life. It is very important to understand that distinction. The faster you can understand that and appreciate it, the better your life and relationships with the guides will be.

Are there evil guides and entities?

There's no question that there is evil energy on this plane – absolutely no question whatsoever. But your spirit guides are the good guys and light always dispels the darkness. When you surround yourself with white light and when you're dealing only with the positive white light energy, you're safe in every single way. But please, for goodness sakes, do not conjure up evil spirits. Do not ask for evil to come into your life. If you pray and ask for white light to surround you, it will dispel all evil and darkness from you. Evil cannot hurt you when you do this.

What is my guide's name?

This is a question that I get asked a lot and the answer really is simple: your guides fundamentally don't care what you call them. I believe some guides will reveal their names to you and I believe that other guides simply want you to give them a name. When parents have a baby, what's that baby's name when it's born? Does it come with a name? No. When a baby is born, the mom and dad get together and give it a name.

I think sometimes people get hung up on the names of their guides. Guides are from Spirit and Spirit really doesn't care what you call them. So, one of the things you can do is either give them a name or allow them to reveal a name to you. Once you've got that, hang on to it. Whatever works best for you is totally okay with them.

How do I know I'm not imagining things or making stuff up?

If you think that your making something up, one of the things you can do is test the answer. If your spirit guides need to get a message delivered to you, it's kind of the same as UPS coming to your door. They ring the doorbell, you don't answer, they leave, then they come back and they try to deliver the package again. They'll continue to do that a couple of times and then they'll leave you a note saying that they tried to deliver it. In other words, they'll make multiple attempts. It's the same with your spirit guides. If your spirit guides need to get a message delivered to you, they're not going to just try once and then give up.

Sometimes messages do come through that may seem unclear. They don't seem to make a lot of sense at the time. So I urge people to have open communication with their guides. If you're confused or you think you're imagining it or you think you just made that up, ask your guides. Your guides don't mind being tested. Tested can sound like a bad word, but testing in this manner is good. You want to validate the information that comes to you.

Let's say you wake up one morning and you feel that you need to quit your job. You're wondering if it's coming from your guides or if it's just frustration and you're tired and you're not sure what to do. You can ask your guides, "Are you sure you're telling me you want me to quit my job?" That's it. Your guides will then give you more messages. They'll continue to keep delivering the messages. Of course, if you don't hear anything back or if they don't try to make a delivery, then let it go. Let it float away. It's as simple as that. Test the messages that you get that are confusing or that you feel you are imagining. Your guides will not be offended. In fact, they'll be thankful because you're paying attention to them.

When your guides talk, is it like your inner voice?

In many ways, yes. The voices that I hear in my head when my guides are actually talking to me is my own inner voice. Don't limit it to any specific method of delivering the message to you. You may hear their voice, you may feel things, you may sense things – be open to all ways of communication.

I did something wrong and I now feel guilty about it. Is that my spirit guides communicating to me?

In many cases, yes. Guilt is a tremendous way for your spirit guides to communicate with you. You probably recall me telling you that your conscience is your guide. Your conscience really is your spirit guides trying to connect to you. You will know when you've done something wrong. I've already shared the example of stealing the gum when I was a little boy and getting away with it. My conscience, aka my spirit guides, never let up when I did that, and they taught me a very valuable lesson.

If you did something wrong and you're feeling guilty about it, guess what? It's because you did something wrong and you need to correct it. For your karma to be clean, you need to go and fix that problem as soon as possible. If you don't, it's likely that guilt is going to get stronger and stronger because your guides tend not to mess with that kind of thing, especially if you did something wrong on purpose or if you did something in a selfish manner. Your guides will help you to get on the right spiritual path, and they will use those feelings to communicate that with you.

Can my spirit guides help me connect with my deceased loved ones?

Yes! Of course they can. One of the biggest keys that I can share with people is this: the key to connecting with your loved ones on the other side is to use your spirit guides as the ambassadors. Let them make the connections for you. It's a wonderful way to have a great relationship with your spirit guides, and your loved ones love using your guides to connect with you. It becomes a terrific relationship and a great way to make those connections. I will be addressing this phenomenon in future books.

FREE Spirit Guide Bridge
Audio Download

If you would like a FREE downloadable audio
recorded by author Blair Robertson designed to easily
and effortlessly help you meet your spirit guides, then
please visit the link below.

BlairRobertson.com/GuidesBonus

About The Author

Blair Robertson is world-renowned psychic medium dedicated to demonstrating that love never dies and that Spirit is all around us. Based in Phoenix, Arizona, he lives with his wife Wendy whom he considers to be the love of his life.

Blair has been featured on the Discovery Channel, Fox News, NBC, ABC, and hundreds of radio shows worldwide. He has produced a number of CDs, DVDs, as well as many free online seminars on spiritual subjects.

Blair Robertson tours widely giving demonstrations of communication with the afterlife. He was once branded a "comedium" by one of his fans for his sense of humor and compassion, Blair excels in delivering messages of love in a loving way.

He has a weekly inspirational newsletter and we invite you to visit and subscribe at

http://www.BlairRobertson.com

Made in the USA
Middletown, DE
12 October 2022